1   Any more for a jolly ride-out in the *Favourite*? A boatman of 1904 with two coy and hesitant passengers

2 *(overleaf)*   A school treat on Bognor sands in 1910 provides eager customers for the beach traders. Tricycles, presumably for hire, are particularly well patronised

Victorian and Edwardian

SUSSEX

from old photographs

Introduction and commentaries by

JAMES S. GRAY

B. T. BATSFORD LTD.

LONDON

First published 1973
Text © James S. Gray 1973

Printed in Great Britain by
William Clowes and Sons Ltd.,
Beccles, Suffolk for the publishers
B. T. Batsford Ltd.,
4 Fitzhardinge Street,
London W1H 0AH

ISBN 0 7134 0131 1

CONTENTS

3 The flower seller rests on a boat beside her basket of posies, c. 1902

ACKNOWLEDGMENTS

The photographs used in this book were drawn from a large variety of sources, libraries, museums, companies, professional photographers and individuals. The Author and Publishers are most grateful, and for the photographs reproduced they wish to thank:

The Marquess of Abergavenny for illustration 94; Milton Adcock: 92; Luther Batchelor: 93, 121, 152; B. T. Batsford Limited: 14, 17, 19, 42, 43, 62, 104, 142; Battle and District Historical Society: 98, 118; Bexhill Museum Association: 13, 15; Miss L. Bishop: 77, 149; A. E. Bissell: 170; Bognor Museum Collection: 39, 111; R. M. Boyd: 97, 150; The Librarian, Brighton Public Library: 4, 51, 113, 115, 134, 141, 154, 155, 159; Wm. Bruford & Son Limited: 18, 135, 164; Mrs K. M. Cawte: 167; Chichester City Museum: 129; C. W. Cramp: 79, 119, 151; T. R. Dadswell: 99, 100; L. S. Davey: 10, 46, 52, 145; The Librarian, Eastbourne Public Library: 20, 21; The Librarian, East Sussex County Library: 55, 87, 114, 138, 161; F. W. Fuller: 89, 90; George Garland: 63, 117, 120, 122, 123, 124, 139, 140, 156, 162, 169; F. M. Goddard: 53; C. W. Goolden: 107; J. S. Gray: 25, 27, 48, 49, 50, 66, 67, 146, 160; Miss F. Greenfield: 76; E. C. Griffith: 71, 72; P. C. Gwynne: 64, 80, 148; The Curator, Hastings Public Museum and Art Gallery: 6, 8, 11, 128; The Librarian, Hastings Public Library: 7, 110; Horsham Museum Society: 78, 133; The Librarian, Hove Public Library: 2, 28, 29, 106; Lancing College: 108; Littlehampton Museum: 33; W. G. Loader: 30, 168; The Mansell Collection: 5, 38, 57; Marlipins Museum, Shoreham: 81, 112; T. Merrett and C. White: 68, 153; Mid-Sussex Times: 144; The Museum of British Transport: 166; N. E. Norris: 22, 95; Mrs K. Pickard-Smith: 45; Reeves Collection, Sunday Times: 23, 54, 59, 83, 84, 85, 86, 88, 116, 125, 127, 132, 143, 147; John Roberts: 65; Aubrey M. Ruff: 1, 3, 9, 12, 58, 105; Rye Museum Association: 101, 102, 103; St Mary's Hall, Brighton: 109; Martin Seymour: 60, 130; H. A. J. Snelling: 82; N. Stephanakis: 96; Sussex Archaeological Society: 44; H. J. F. Thompson: 37, 56, 131; Valentines of Dundee Limited: 24, 26, 41; Jack Watts: 34, 35, 36, 61, 136, 157; The Librarian, West Sussex County Library: 69, 75; The County Archivist, West Sussex County Record Office: 70, 73, 74; Mrs M. E. Winchester: 16, 91, 137, 165; The Librarian, Worthing Public Library: 31, 32; Gerard Young Collection (now at Bognor College of Education): 40, 47, 126, 158, 163.

The Author could not have gathered the factual information on which the commentaries are based without the valued help willingly provided by the staffs of public libraries and museums throughout the county. In particular, he gratefully acknowledges the assistance of Miss E. Baird, Miss B. Greenhill and Miss E. Hollingdale (of Brighton Reference Library), Miss M. Lewis (of Eastbourne Public Library), Miss L. M. Green (of Hove Reference Library), Mr R. Adderley (of East Sussex County Library), Mr D. R. Elleray (of Worthing Reference Library), Mrs P. Gill and Dr G. J. Mead (of West Sussex County Record Office), Mr G. Manwaring Baines (Curator, Hastings Public Museum and Art Gallery) and Mr H. J. Sargent (Curator, Bexhill Museum). Facts and dates were verified for him by the Editors of the Mid-Sussex Times and the West Sussex Gazette, for which they are thanked.

The Author is also deeply indebted to those individuals mentioned in the Acknowledgments, who not only provided the photographs, but often also contributed information for the commentaries from their specialised local knowledge. They are too many for their names to be repeated, but for exceptional help mention must be made of Mr G. Garland, Mr N. E. Norris and Mr Jack Watts. In addition thanks are due to Mr K. W. Astell, Mr B. Austen, Mr G. S. Bagley, Mr D. Buckman, Mr Bob Copper, Mr F. J. Hunt, Mr M. Leppard, Mr A. F. Payne and Mr F. H. Witten, for factual information about many of the photographs.

Finally the Author wishes to thank Mr Tom Scott, for his sustained help and encouragement, and Mr John Barrow of Hove, for his work in reproducing the photographs. Quotations in the commentaries are from local newspapers of the period.

4 The 'Cinderella' Coach drawn by three goats, a popular feature of the sea front scene of 1906

INTRODUCTION

I first visited Sussex when I was a child in the early years of the 1914–1918 war; my only recollection is of getting into a horse bus outside Brighton station. In the last year of that war I was sent by my parents to spend the school summer holiday with friends in Brighton and my spartan father decreed that I should travel down from South London on my newly acquired bicycle. The journey was uneventful as there was little traffic about, the only hazard to me being the gritty road which caused frequent punctures. Soon after descending Handcross Hill and near to Bolney, at a bend in the road, I saw for the first time the long stretch of the South Downs. In my boyish imagination I saw them as a sleeping pride of lions through which I had to thread my way to reach the coast. The journey took me six hours.

In the Brighton of 1918 there was little for an active boy to do except swim, cycle or walk. Soon tiring of the sea I took to the Downs on foot, exploring the area from north of Hangleton in the west to Ditchling Beacon in the east. Remember that this was in the days before the twentieth-century agricultural revolution, when man shared the Downs with the sheep, the lark and the grayling butterfly. I found the serene pool at Poynings, now long since gone through silting up, and took the long way back to Hove by walking the full length of the Dyke Railway track, closed to traffic for the duration of the war. Above Patcham I met an old shepherd, glad even of a boy's company, who told me stories of how wheatears were snared on the Downs in his younger days, and of dewponds and where to find them. Two years later I was one of eight schoolboys who volunteered to join two masters in an all-night 'stroll' from East Croydon station to Brighton. After 12 weary hours this ended ingloriously as I rode the last five miles into Brighton, wedged between milk churns on a horse-drawn farm cart. This, then, was my introduction to Sussex. In 1923 I moved to the Brighton area where I have lived ever since.

When Victoria ascended the throne on 20 June 1837 there was no railway in Sussex, but one of Her Majesty's first acts, on 15 July, was to give Royal assent to the Bill for the construction of the London to Brighton line. Brighton, the only sizeable town in the county (1841 population – 46,661) had been stagnating after losing the stimulus provided by the patronage of George IV. The other resorts along the Sussex coast were much smaller, not only in size but in population as well. James Burton's St Leonards had been built and was governed by Commissioners, but had not yet joined, physically or administratively, the neighbouring town of Hastings. To the west, Worthing was slowly developing and had its own Town Hall. Roads through the country areas into these towns were controlled by turnpike trusts, mostly set up in the second half of the eighteenth century. These provided a road surface good enough for the regular passage of coaches, but the modest tolls of the turnpikes, which affected farmers and merchants as well as pleasure travellers, added to the cost of living. The secondary country roads were little more than tracks of flint and grit. Producing dust in summer and thick mud in winter, they nevertheless had to be used by most inhabitants to get from one village to another. Sussex had no heavy industry. Iron making had gone before photography could record it. Brighton's loco-motive works had yet to be built. In the country areas men were born, grew up, worked chiefly on the land, reared their families and died, without venturing far from their birthplace.

As the Queen's reign lengthened the scene changed due principally to the advent of the railway. From 1840 onwards its tentacles spread across the whole face of Sussex, opening up the county by improved communications, the growth of trade and the movement of population. Not only did it provide employment, at first during its construction and later for its staff, but it encouraged country labour to seek higher wages in the coastal towns, which in turn increased in popularity as the railway travellers poured in. Between 1841 and 1861 Brighton's population grew by 31,032 to 77,693! Although the railway killed the coach trade almost at once and the turnpike trusts a little later, the country carrier (Fig. 121) prospered. In 1868 Brighton had 31 carriers making regular journeys to 56 towns and villages in the county. Victoria's Jubilees came and went and by the time her son succeeded her the railway network was almost complete. County and municipal boroughs

5 The *Worthing Belle* at Nelson Steps, 1908. The Arun windmill was built in 1831 and was working until 1913. It was removed in 1931

had been formed, and the rest of the county administratively split into East and West Sussex. The motor car had arrived, and been emancipated, and during Edward's brief reign Sussex was to see its first aeroplane.

The photographs reflect some of these changes, but not all. The choice of subject for a Victorian photographer was not always his own. Often he took pictures of general interest for subsequent sale; also he was employed to take a particular photograph. (Fig. 91 seems a likely example of this.) Edward Fox's visit to Mayfield from Brighton in 1864, with all his equipment, must have been quite a journey. Again, the populous towns and particularly the sea fronts, promenades and beaches of the resorts, attracted the most attention. Here could be found the fashionables, and the not-so-fashionables, to be photographed according to the whim of the individual. Fortunately not all photographers ignored the *hoi polloi*. Of course location often determined the character of the pictures. The scenes photographed on Hastings beach could well have been repeated at Brighton or Bognor, but hardly, at that period, in Eastbourne or Hove. In these towns the camera was focussed on solid, middle-class citizens perambulating and gossiping on the Parades and Lawns, or listening to the band.

In the country, concentration seems to have been upon the village street, the High Street, often the only street of any importance. Here were the few shops, the church, the school. Some of these High Streets are little changed today apart from having better roads and pavements, improvements lessened by the ever increasing flow of traffic. The patriotic fervour of the times is mirrored in the scenes of the Jubilee and Coronation celebrations, the royal visits and the Volunteer Parades. The later branches and stations of the railway were well photographed; the size of the staffs at country stations suggests a busy activity with passengers and freight; the goods yard a focal point as coal for household use and the local gas works was discharged, and as agricultural machines and implements were unloaded. There are no photographs of slums, which is not to say that they did not exist. The jibe that Brighton had its 'Queen Anne front and Mary Ann back' contained more than a germ of truth. It is to the credit of Brighton Corporation that they swept away some of these hovels in the 'seventies and still more in the 'nineties, but others remained. Slums were not a subject for discussion in polite society and photographers had no reason to venture into these areas. Certainly there would have been no sale for their photographs.

People bring pictures to life; without them this book would be just an impersonal record of changes in the face of town and country. And yet, as we look at these folk, we know almost nothing of their lives, their hopes, their fears. Their expressionless faces give no clue to their thoughts and their feelings. Certainly they enjoyed being photographed, either as principals or background material, with few of the self-conscious antics displayed by present-day television crowds. The picture which emerges is of an industrious, hard-working people, dressed for the most part in shabby solemnity; taking life seriously, for there is scarcely a smile to be seen on any face, and disciplined to the conventions of the period. For example, it seems to have been taboo for a man to appear out-of-doors with his head uncovered by hat or cap. They appeared to relax only on the rare occasion of a trip to the seaside or village fair, but were determined to make the most of any unexpected public holiday provided by a royal event. Victorian roads, even in the towns, seem coated with mud and dirt, and bespattered with horse and cattle manure. After the turn of the century wood blocking and the introduction of tarmac improved the surfaces. Note, though, the almost complete absence of litter. Money was scarce and after the rent had been paid it was spent on little else than food, drink, fuel and clothing; the people had not much to throw down in the streets even had they felt so inclined. Present-day litter is a by-product of the affluent society.

Finding these photographs was not difficult, but involved a great deal of travel. Sussex is a broad county; the distance from Rye to Bosham is considerable. Starting with the premise that ideally all towns and villages should be represented I soon found that there were far more photographs of the coastal resorts than of the country areas. Public libraries and museums in these large towns were here the main source; indeed there were so many available that ruthless pruning was needed to keep those chosen to a reasonable number. A fair balance had to be struck between coast and interior. Brighton and Hove, the largest conurbation, receive only token representation as they have been adequately portrayed in an earlier book.* In some country towns there were many photographs. Lewes and Petworth are good examples, while as would be expected, picturesque Rye has an abundance of fascinating early photographs. In other places I found people who had painstakingly built up collections of local photographs, and who readily let me choose from these. In this way I have been able to show scenes from about 60 towns, villages and places in the county, the photographs having been drawn from 58 sources. I am well aware that many places are not shown. To their inhabitants I can only plead the sheer physical impossibility of visiting every town and searching for photographs, coupled with the limitation on the total number to be used.

In conclusion I would like to commend the excellence of the work of some mid-Victorian photographers. They had some advantages, including plenty of time and little disturbance from traffic. They could set up their equipment and wait until conditions were just right. Given all this, however, they produced photographs of remarkable quality. Consider the clarity and sharpness of Fig. 83 by Lewes photographer, Edward Reeves (1824–1905). Could this be bettered today?

JAMES S. GRAY
January, 1973

* John Betjeman and J. S. Gray, *Victorian and Edwardian Brighton from Old Photographs*

The Coastal Resorts

HASTINGS

6 The bathing machines opposite Carlisle Parade and Robertson Terrace, *c.* 1900. The sexes were segregated, the mens' bathing machines in the forefront with the ladies' on the beach beyond. In the distance, the skeleton of the harbour arm

7   The St Leonards sea front in 1864. At the left is the Royal Victoria Hotel with its main entrance at the rear. Opened in October 1829 as the St Leonards Hotel, it was renamed after the royal visit of 1834. The low building behind the bathing machines was the Baths. St Leonards was amalgamated with Hastings in 1885

8   A refreshing paddle at low tide in the summer of 1901. A glimpse of Hastings Castle is visible on the hill beyond

9 A street scene in the Old Town, 1900. Children are drinking from the pump which stood against the wall of Breeds Brewery in Bourne Walk. In 1835, when the bed of the old Bourne Stream was covered in, this pump was provided for public use

10 Hastings Old Town, the fishing fleet and the wooden net shops on the Stade, seen from the East Cliff in the 1870's. The brig *Pelican* seen here was built at Hastings in 1838. A collier, she landed her coals on the open beach and was in service for 40 years until broken up about 1880

11 An Edwardian 'knees-up' at the foot of Cambridge Road in 1902 attracts the attention of youthful bystanders, but older people seem disinterested

12 A girl swinging on the rigging of the *Flying Fish*, 1903. Just to the right of the net shops is the Fishermen's Church. Built in 1854, it is now the Fishermen's Museum

13 Bexhill in 1886. From the Coastguard Station looking east, showing the first few houses built to the south of the railway. The Devonshire Hotel is the facing building in the centre

BEXHILL

14 *(right)* The cycle boulevard on the East Parade in 1896, the year in which it was opened. It was half a mile long and admission was a modest 2d. The first motor races in England were held here in 1902. The low circular building opposite the Sackville Hotel was the cycle chalet where bicycles could be hired

15 *(below)* The early days of West Parade, *c.* 1900. The photograph was taken from the low cliff later occupied by the Colonnade

16   Looking east from the Pier to Splash Point and Marine Parade, 1868. The Field House *(left)* was pulled down in 1877 and replaced by the Queens Hotel, opened in 1881. The boats were a later addition to the original photograph

EASTBOURNE

17   A profusion of bathing machines in this 1898 photograph of the beach and sea front, from the Wish Tower as far as the Pier and Queens Hotel. The parade had been freshly watered by the water cart

18 Eastbourne Station and Terminus Road, in the 1870's. Terminus Road was laid out in 1849/50 by the Gilbert Estate. Before the railway reached Eastbourne on 14 May 1849 the horse bus used to take passengers to Polegate Station, there to connect with the Hastings–London trains

19 The late-Victorian scene on Grand Parade, just opposite the Cavendish Hotel, in 1898. The bandstand, built a few years earlier, was replaced by the present one on the same site in 1934. The kerbside railing has now gone, though a small part remains by the gardens near the Pier

20 Chapman's horse bus on Eastbourne front, about 1890. Chapman and Son ran a town horse-bus service, and excursions into the countryside, from the early 1880's. Here the bus is standing outside the entrance to the Pier

21 The 2nd Sussex Artillery Volunteers encamped at Eastbourne Redoubt in the late 1890's. The Redoubt was built at the same time as the Martello Towers, as part of the defence system against Napoleon, and was occupied by the military on and off until about 1900. It was conveyed to Eastbourne Corporation in 1925

22 Beachy Head Lighthouse under construction, 1901. Work started in 1899 and finished in 1902. It replaced the Belle Tout light and was brought into operation on 2 October 1902

SEAFORD

23 Seaford beach looking east, *c.* 1870. The shingle bar was badly breached in 1875 and this led to the building of the Esplanade and sea wall in 1881. The small building on the beach was occupied as the Assembly Rooms and Baths; beyond is Corsica Hall, rebuilt in 1823 and now Seaford College of Education

24 Kings Road, the Western Esplanade and the Gardens, 1891. These enclosures were laid out in 1884 and replaced by the present lawns and boating pool in 1925/26. At the left the Bedford Hotel, opened in 1829 and destroyed by fire on 1 April 1964

25 A meeting of the Croquet Club on the east lawn of the Royal Pavilion, *c.* 1875

26 Part of the fishing fleet on the central beach, 1891

27 Brighton beach, from just east of the West Pier to the distant Chain Pier. The year is 1889, when one of the stone groynes, which so built up the beach, was being constructed. The Grand Hotel can be seen, but the nearby Metropole had yet to be built

28 Genteel Hove. Sunday morning church parade on the Brunswick Lawns, 1905. This feature of Hove's social life reached its zenith in Edwardian days

HOVE

29 The horse bus bound for Castle Square, Brighton, at its terminus in New Church Road, c. 1900. This bus linked up with the horse tramway to Shoreham, the rails of which can be seen. A peculiarity was that at this terminus it stood at the off side of the road, not its near side

30   The scene on the sea front, looking east, following the floods of New Year's Day, 1877. Taken from the Royal Hotel, showing the sea flooding into South Street. During the 1870's the sea overflowed into the streets on many occasions

WORTHING

31   The Royal Hotel and South Street from the Pier, in 1884. Formerly the Sea House, later Royal Sea House Hotel, it was built about 1824 and destroyed by fire on 21 May 1901. The Pier was built by Sir Robert Rawlinson. 960 feet long and 15 feet wide, it was opened on 12 April 1862

32 Crowds on Worthing beach for the celebration of Queen Victoria's Golden Jubilee, 21 June 1887. The chief event was the launching of the lifeboat *Henry Harris* followed by races between members of local rowing clubs in four-oared galleys. It was reported that 'fully ten thousand people were assembled'

33   South Street and the Old Town Hall, *c.* 1905. The Town Hall (built in 1834/5) served Worthing for a century until replaced by the present one in May 1933. The old building lingered on until June 1966. The canvas blinds *(right)* were hung on hooks at the top of the shop fascia and pulled over the horizontal iron rail. This passed through eyes in the vertical rods which fixed into slots in the pavement

34 A procession advertising Sangers Circus in Chapel Road, about 1905. The narrow roadway was widened by several feet being taken from the broad pavement *(right)* in 1906

35 High Street in 1893 during the outbreak of typhoid fever which lasted from June until November. The water supply became contaminated from an old disused sewer and householders had to obtain pure drinking water from tanks such as the one shown. The Swan Inn *(extreme left)* is still there, as is the house, The Hollies, hidden behind the trees

LITTLEHAMPTON

36 A village street, within the borough, soon after the turn of the century. Broadwater Street West, now a busy shopping thoroughfare, remained like this until the late 1920's, after which alterations and road widening completely transformed its appearance

37 High Street, looking east, *c.* 1880. The low cottage buildings *(right)* were removed soon afterwards and Clifton Road cut through here in 1885. On the opposite side the Classic Cinema was built in 1931 on the site shielded by the high brick wall. The distant St Mary's Church was rebuilt in 1934

38 The ferry across the Arun, in 1908. The Ferry Act was passed in 1824 and a wooden barge built, later replaced by a steel pontoon. The bridge which replaced the ferry was opened by the Duke of Norfolk on 27 May 1908

39 An early photograph of the eastern beaches, from the Pier, c. 1870. The distant tall buildings were those of Colebrook Terrace, later a school and demolished in 1947. The low sea wall is draped with fishing nets

BOGNOR

40 How ladies bathed at Bognor in the 1880's. Bathing machines being towed to and from the sea at low tide. Taken from the Pier, the photograph shows Waterloo Square and houses on the Esplanade, some of which have since been removed probably when the Royal Hotel was built

41 High Street, looking west from York Road, in 1898. Adjoining the residential property on the north side is Bognor's first Methodist Chapel. The weighing machine *(right)* stands on the forecourt of the Anchor Inn. The early car attracts some attention.

42 Peaceful Upper Bognor Road, in 1903. It is now a part of the busy A.259

The Farming Scene

43 A shepherd with his dog and flock of Southdown sheep on the Downs near Eastbourne, *c*. 1910. The worn patches of grassland show where temporary sheep folds have been

44 Striking a bargain. Lewes Sheep Fair on the Racecourse, 1891

46 *(right)* Haymaking with a team of oxen near Lewes, *c.* 1900. The ox goad held by the lad was a hazel stick about nine feet long with an iron spur

45 *(below)* Threshing at New Barn, Home Farm, Glynde, September, 1907

47 A group of farm workers at Church Farm, Pagham in 1881. They sport a fine variety of head-gear; not one man or boy is without a hat

48 Loading faggots at Longhouse Farm, Cowfold, 16 June 1891

49 Gleaners in the fields at Southwick, 23 August 1892. After the stooks had been removed the gleaners, often the wives and children of the farm workers, were allowed to pick up what was left: a useful addition to their food

50 Putting in the ferret. Boys rabbiting at Hempstead, Framfield, 2 September 1894.
The fox terrier is very much on the alert

51 Shoeing an ox at Saddlescombe Farm. First the animal was roped and borne to the ground. Then its feet were tied to a brake trave – three pieces of wood hinged in the form of a triangle – before it could be shod. The smallest boy sat on the animal's neck

The Harbours
and Rivers

52 A sprit-rigged barge from Lewes on the Ouse bound for Newhaven to load coals for Lewes merchants, c. 1890. In the background are the Downs, with Mount Caburn on the extreme right

53 View across Shoreham Harbour from the east, *c.* 1890. Kingston Pier, dividing the east and west arms, was constructed about 1820. It was lengthened when the lighthouse was built in 1846

54 Newhaven Harbour, *c.* 1870. The colliers moored against the pier were part of the fleet of John Bull, Newhaven's chief shipowner. Behind them is the London and Paris Hotel, built in 1847/48 after the coming of the railway and demolished in 1958

55 The reconstruction and extension of Newhaven Harbour, December 1879. Men are working on the construction of the sea wall to enclose a large area later filled in with materials from the cliffs. When this wall was finished the present breakwater on the west side was built out from Barrow Head

56 Littlehampton Harbour, looking upstream, *c.* 1900, showing the paddle tug *Jumna* and three brigantines. In the foreground are two coastguards with their double-ended lifeboat

57 Hastings Harbour arm decorated for the laying of the foundation stone on 16 June 1897. It was to have been 1700 feet long, but the builders encountered a deep depression filled with mud across which the breakwater would have to run. This proved impossible to fill, to provide a secure foundation, so the project was abandoned

62   The ferry across the Arun at Bury, *c.* 1902. The 'right of ferry', to charge for conveying passengers, was held by the Duke of Norfolk. It was closed in 1957, but its location is easily found. The barn in the centre has been replaced by a house and the view towards the church is now obscured

63 One of the last barges on the Arun Navigation, near Pulborough, *c.* 1885. Henry Doick, barge-master, is in No. 64. The Navigation existed for just over 100 years, from 1787 until its closure on 1 January 1888

68 MIDHURST The peaceful scene in North Street, then mainly residential, in the 1870's. Several of the houses on the left near the lamp post were removed for the Town Hall, built in 1882. At the right, the Angel Hotel

West Sussex

73 ARUNDEL Looking up High Street, *c.* 1870. The central column was the town pump which raised water from Hamper's Well; it was presented to the town in 1834 by Lord Dudley Coutts Stuart, M.P. It was removed in 1921 to make way for the War Memorial

74 ARUNDEL The rebuilding of Arundel Castle in progress. This extensive work occupied the years 1890–1903

75 MIDHURST Patients at lunch in the dining room of the King Edward VII Sanatorium, 1908. This hospital for consumptives was built as the result of a gift of £200,000 by Sir Ernest Cassel

76 STORRINGTON Church Street in 1868, showing at the right James Greenfield's shop with bales of drugget and straw bee-skeps. On the opposite side the house occupied by Duke, Shoeing Smith, is still named Forge Cottage

80 CRAWLEY   Announcing the result of the Horsham Parliamentary Election, 26 January 1910.
This was made from the Railway Hotel, High Street. Earl Winterton (Conservative) won the seat
with 6,324 votes and this was the start of his long association with the constituency

81 SHOREHAM High Street from the west, 1878. At the extreme right is the Crown and Anchor Hotel. The lamp post outside the Brewery was formerly one of ten columns which supported the Market House; this faced the Crown and Anchor and was removed in 1823

82 SHOREHAM A parade of the Sussex Artillery Volunteers at Kingston Redoubt (Shoreham Fort), c. 1896. Formed at Brighton in 1859, the Volunteers fired in practice from Newhaven Fort as well as at Shoreham. All ranks are wearing blue cloth full-dress uniform

East Sussex

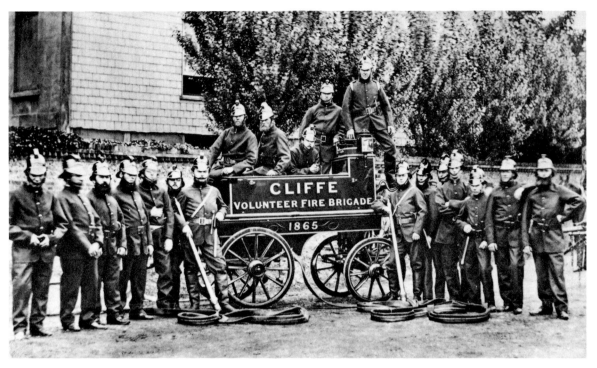

84 LEWES   Members of Cliffe Volunteer Fire Brigade, with appliance and leather riveted hose, *c*. 1870. Their Headquarters were in Cliffe Square behind the Church of St Thomas à Beckett. Cliffe was incorporated with Lewes in 1881

83 LEWES   School Hill, 1875. A remarkably clear photograph which shows this street little different from today other than the levelling of the severely cambered roadway. The distant building resembling a church is Undercliff House, still approached from Malling Street only by a footpath

85 A Victorian family ensemble, 1870. The exact location is not known but it is thought to have been within a mile or two of Lewes

86 NEWHAVEN The narrow gas-lit High Street, with cobbled footways, 1866. Looking down towards the river. The Blue Anchor Inn dated from 1762. Almost opposite is the White Hart, set back in 1922 when the street was widened

87   BISHOPSTONE   The Tide Mills, August 1883. Here was the largest water mill in Sussex, in use for 16 hours a day. The windmill was used for hoisting grain to the granary. In William Catt's time as miller (1803–1853) this became a self-contained village, with mill-house, workers' cottages and three gates which were locked each night at 10 o'clock

88 UCKFIELD A quiet part of the High Street, looking north in 1873. It is seemingly a very warm day as the few people about have sought the shade

90 *(overleaf)* UCKFIELD A Bristol biplane makes a forced landing in a field near the Recreation Ground, 1910. The pilot escaped without injury

89 UCKFIELD Collapse of the road bridge carrying the London–Eastbourne traffic, now the A.22, 27 June 1903. This bridge, close to the Railway Station, was built in 1858 at a cost of £500, to replace an old stone three-arch bridge

91 MAYFIELD Ruins of the Archbishop's Palace, photographed by Edward Fox of Brighton, 1864. Built about 1325, it was in this derelict state when bought by the Duchess of Leeds in 1863. She gave it to the Foundress of the Society of the Holy Child Jesus, on condition that the ruins be restored. This work started on 19 May 1864. It is now the Convent chapel

92 HEATHFIELD The station lit by natural gas, 1903. Discovered in 1896 the gas was also supplied to a few houses and used for street lighting. Efforts were made to develop it commercially but with little success. The gasometer was removed when this stretch of railway was closed in 1965

93 CROWBOROUGH High Street in 1880, looking towards the Crowborough Cross Hotel and the cross-roads. It has since been almost completely rebuilt as a busy shopping street, though parts of the wall *(left)* and the distant barn building are still there

94 ERIDGE A family group on the croquet lawn at Eridge Castle, *c.* 1860. The Rev. The Earl of Abergavenny and his wife are in the centre. The group also includes the 1st Marquess of Abergavenny, his wife and their three sons, The Earl of Lewes *(centre)*, Lord Henry Nevill *(right)*, and Lord Richard Nevill *(left)*

95 LINDFIELD The Thatched Cottage, and beyond, what is now the west wing of Old Place. Period about 1865/70. Today the front garden of the Cottage extends across, and has obliterated, the rough track in front of the buildings

96 EAST GRINSTEAD High Street, from near to the junction with London Road, *c.* 1890. Now the busy A.22

97 ALFRISTON   The 1885 view along the west side of High Street, showing *(left)* the Steamer public house, long since closed, though the houses are now known as Steamer Cottages. Beyond is the famous Star Inn, built in 1520

98 BATTLE High Street and Caldbec Hill, from the top of the Abbey Gateway. On the distant ridge are two windmills. The Black Mill *(left)* was burned down in 1872 so the photograph dates from before then

99 ROBERTSBRIDGE The old flour mill, *c.* 1865. The mill stream was a man-made cut from the Rother, near Etchingham. The mill was demolished and rebuilt in 1878. The house still exists though altered and extended

100 ROBERTSBRIDGE A waggonette, with four horses postillion-ridden, meeting, probably, a house party at Robertsbridge Station, in the 1870's. Their destination is not known. The station was opened in 1851 and has since been much extended

101 WINCHELSEA The Court Hall and Wesley's tree, 1860. It is reported that under this ash tree John Wesley ended his great open-air ministry on 7 October 1790. The Court Hall now houses Winchelsea Museum

102 RYE The town side of the Landgate, looking north from Hilders Cliff, *c.* 1860: probably the best remaining part of the old walled fortifications. The clock was placed in Landgate tower in 1863, in memory of the Prince Consort

103 RYE The entrance to Mermaid Passage in 1890. The passageway has now been restored to its original width, when it was the way-in for coaches. The entrance on the left now leads to the office of the Mermaid Hotel

104 RYE Old houses in The Mint, *c.* 1888. Three of four adjoining houses were Inns; of these only the Standard now remains. Note the paving set into the cobbled street to ease the passage of horse traffic

105 RYE Looking up Mermaid Street, 1901

Schools

106 Sarah Robinson's school at Crawley, 1866. This was the British School, opened in October 1854, largely as the result of the efforts of Mrs Robinson of Crawley Manor House. The original schoolroom and adjoining master's house were built at a total cost of £510. It was demolished in 1916

107 *(above)* Hammerwood School near East Grinstead, *c.* 1905. This was built (1872) to the design of Norman Shaw; the ivy-clad building was a chapel. The tower was removed in the 1930's. The school closed in 1957 and the building has been converted to three private houses

108 Lancing College, from Shoreham toll-bridge, 1875, showing the completed dining hall and the chapel *(right)* up to crypt level. It is suggested that the south wall of the dining hall is the largest area of split-flint facing in the country. Designed by R. C. Carpenter, the College was opened in 1858

109 The cloisters at St Mary's Hall, Brighton, 1890's. Founded by the Rev. H. V. Elliott as a School for the Daughters of the Clergy, it was opened on 1 August 1836. The architect was George Basevi. The cloisters were for 'recreation in wet weather'; they were removed when the School Hall was built in 1910

Sussex Industries

110 FISHING An 1864 photograph of fishermen making nets beneath the East Cliff, Hastings. The gas lamp stands in Rock-a-Nore Road

111 CHARCOAL BURNING A family of charcoal burners in Arundel Park in the 1900's, showing caravan, storage hut and charcoal heap

112 SHIPBUILDING The barque *Brittania* under construction at Dyer's Yard, Shoreham, in 1877. She had a short, but busy, life of only six years, being lost at sea in 1883

113 TRUG MAKING Trug maker at Rotherfield, about 1900. This industry started in Sussex about 1840, chestnut being used for the frame with willow slats. So that they could be bent the chestnut strips were first placed in a steam oven for 15 minutes

114 *(overleaf)* LOCOMOTIVE BUILDING 2–4–0 locomotive 690, built at Brighton Railway Works. Here, in November 1883, it is being hoisted on board the *Viking* at Newhaven, en route to the Paris Exhibition. The tender rests on the rails below

The Working Day

115   Knife grinders at work in Sheffield Park, 1891

116   Road works in High Street, Lewes, in 1875 attract the interest of bystanders determined to get in the photograph. The men are outside the shop of J. Shelley, Miller and Baker. Part of this building, which still stands by St Martins Lane, dates from the fourteenth century

117 A group of Petworth Prison staff in 1880. The House of Correction was built in 1788; when Horsham Gaol was given up in 1843 it became the prison for the Western Division of the County. It was demolished in 1881

118 *(below, left)* The donkey milkman in Upper Lake, Battle, *c.* 1908. Skim milk was then ½d a pint. The central house and that hidden from view behind the garden railing, are now a motor garage and showroom

119 *(below right)* The Horsham postman of 1850

120 Preparing the evening meal at Burton House, near Petworth, *c.* 1895. *From left to right* – the cook, under kitchenmaid, kitchenmaid and footman. Since 1946 Burton House has been occupied by St Michael's School for Girls

121 The country carrier with his horse and van in High Street, Crowborough, 1890. Thomas Jarvis made the journey from Crowborough to London each Tuesday, returning from the Queens Head Inn on Wednesdays

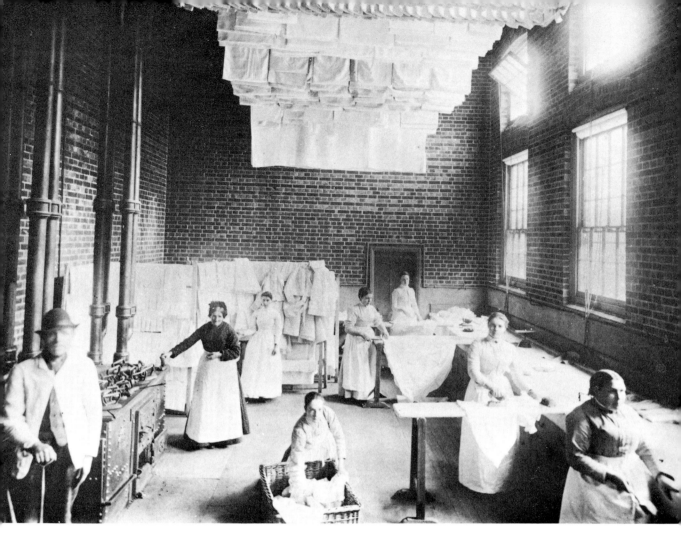

122 The laundry at Petworth House, *c.* 1890

123 The South Downs provide an unusual background to the Duncton hearse of the 1890's. The driver, James Hampton, was also the local wheelwright

124 One whose working days perhaps were over.
Photographed in 1880 outside Bignor Church, this old man
was born in 1800. Described in the church register as a
labourer and day labourer, he is wearing a black Sussex
round frock. A white smock was worn on Sundays

Shops and Markets

125   A Christmas display at Coppard's, 53, High Street, Lewes, 1878

126 Henry Lovett's shop, 61/63, High Street, Bognor in the 1870's. In addition to his stationery and fancy goods business he was the founder of the *Bognor Observer*, first published on 1 May 1872; the paper was printed in Lennox Street at the rear of this shop

127 A fine array of cheeses at Jenner's shop, 3, North Street, Lewes, in 1880. The shop front and fine doorway have since been replaced, but the adjoining buildings are little changed. The corner house still retains its upstairs bow window and facing black mathematical tiles

128 Fish auction at Hastings Fishmarket, 1900. Behind the stooping man is the hand-wheel of the ice crushing machine. The wooden structure in the centre is the gallows on which lights were hung to guide in the fishing fleet at night

129 The Cattle Market in Eastgate Square, Chichester, 1869. This extended along East Street and, by the Cross, into North Street; the Cattle Market Inn took its name from this. The permanent enclosed market was opened on 10 May 1871

130 Steyning Market, when it was held in the High Street, *c*. 1885. At the extreme left is the White Horse Hotel, partially destroyed by fire in 1949. The curly-brimmed hats were called felt hats and were quite cheap, costing about two shillings new and sixpence second-hand

131 Norfolk Hotel, Surrey Street Littlehampton, *c.* 1860. At one time a regular coach ran from here to The White Horse, Fetter Lane, London. Among notable visitors were Col. Shrapnel (1761–1842), who had a work-shop just off East Street, and Dr. Aber-nethy of biscuit fame. Built early in the nineteenth century, the hotel was demolished in 1959

Inns

132   The Bridge Inn, Newhaven, 1867, when the landlord was Charles Cooke. It was built as the New Inn in 1623, and renamed about 1793 after the opening of the nearby drawbridge. The wall inscriptions record the brief stay of King Louis Philippe and his Queen on their escape from France in March 1848. At the extreme left is the old drawbridge toll-house

133 The Lamb Inn, Carfax, Horsham, 1855. In the window is a mention of 'good beds'

134 The Bull Inn, Mockbridge, Shermanbury, c. 1885. When the present inn was built, a few yards away, in 1893 the old building was converted to separate cottages, demolished just a few years ago

135 The Terminus Hotel, Eastbourne in the 1860's. Sited at the junction of Terminus Road *(foreground)*, Grove Road and Ivy Terrace. Before the railway opened in 1849 it was Hartfield Farm House

Manners and Customs

136 Sompting May Day Procession, 1908, headed west and passing Yew Tree Farm. This custom started in 1864. Children on holiday from school proceeded to Sompting Abbotts; after Maypole and Morris dancing they were entertained to tea. A collection in the village reached £4–1–7, which was given to the children

137 Fair Day in Mayfield High Street, 1890's. The fair was held twice a year, on May 13 and November 13

138 East Grinstead Fair in the High Street, 21 April 1896. The right to hold a fair was granted by Royal Charter in 1247. The December Fair continued until the early 1930's; the others in April, July and September had died out previously

139 Dancing around the Maypole, on the Rectory lawn, at Petworth Rectory Fête, 1900. Petworth Town Band is in attendance

140 *(below left)* Lord Leconfield's Club Procession, with the Petworth Park Friendly Society banner, June 1907. They are on their way to a service at Petworth church, to be followed by the Club Dinner at Petworth Park

141 *(below)* Ebernoe Horn Fair, 25 July 1908: a custom which is still observed today. A sheep is roasted and the horns are given to the batsman with the highest score in the cricket match played on the same day

142 Glorious Goodwood. The racecourse, stands and Trundle Hill, July 1903

Sport and Recreation

143 A day with the guns, *c.* 1880. Putting together the 'bag' in a spinney near Lewes

144 The start of the cycle race from Friars Oak Inn, May 1893. The course was to Stonepound, Hassocks, Keymer, Ditchling Common, Keymer Junction and via St John's Common back to the Inn, about 9 miles. No. 6 was the winner in 32 minutes, 17 seconds, No. 2 on his 'penny-farthing' finishing a creditable fourth. The road from Ditchling across the common was 'rough with stones'

145   Lewes Roller Skating Rink, gas lit and festooned with chinese lanterns, *c.* 1879. It was located at the Lewes and County Club, High Street, St Annes, opened in 1877

146   A family game of stoolball near Bolney, 8 June 1891

147 *(overleaf)*   Lady croquet players on the seventeenth-century Old Lewes Bowling Green, in Castle Precincts, *c.* 1870. The wooden pavilion still exists today

148 E. F. Broad, winner of the first Stock Exchange, London to Brighton walk, passing through Crawley, 1 May 1903. Wearing 'a close-fitted woollen costume of dark blue' he finished in 9 hours, 30 minutes, 1 second. Rain made the already bad roads even worse and he reached Brighton Aquarium with his 'legs plastered in solid mud up to the knees'

149 Henfield Cricket Club, players and spectators, on Henfield Common, 1864. Founded in 1772 as Henfield Club, it was reconstituted in May 1837, with very strict rules. The club has always played on the Common, where the present pavilion was opened on 19 July 1926

150 A marbles match in Waterloo Square, Alfriston, 1900. Troops who later fought at Waterloo were stationed in this row of cottages, hence the name. The market cross, which dates from 1833, was built smaller than the one it replaced because of traffic congestion!

Public Occasions

151 West Street, Horsham decorated for the Queen's Golden Jubilee: a public holiday with all schools closed, 20 June 1887

152 Crowborough prepares for the Diamond Jubilee. The Bonfire Beacon was 60 feet in height; the materials used included 100 railway sleepers, 3000 faggots, 100 gallons of tar and a barrel of paraffin. It is said that 94 such beacons were lit in Sussex on the night of 22 June 1897

153 The arrival of King Edward and Queen Alexandra at Midhurst (L.B. & S.C.R.) station, 13 June 1906. The guard of honour was provided by the 2nd Volunteer Battalion, Royal Sussex Regiment. The purpose of their visit was the opening of the King Edward VII Sanatorium

154 The scene outside Woolavington Church, 25 July 1873, as mourners assembled for the funeral of Dr Samuel Wilberforce, Bishop of Winchester. He was lord of the manor of this parish and had lived close to the church. A special train from London brought 250 people, including several bishops

155 Schoolchildren in procession along Westham Street on 9 August 1902, the day of King Edward VII's Coronation. They are on their way to the service at St Mary's Parish Church, Westham, Pevensey

156 Petworth Town Band forming up outside the Cricketers Inn, Duncton, at the time of the Coronation, 1902. They were soon to move off on the journey to Burton Park. In this exclusively male gathering none is without a hat or cap

157 Launching the lifeboat, *Richard Coleman*, from the beach east of Worthing Pier, 7 August 1901. The other lifeboats seen are those from Littlehampton and Shoreham; also an earlier Worthing boat, the *Henry Harris*

158 Looking east along High Street, Bognor, en fête for the visit of the Duke and Duchess of York (later King George V and Queen Mary). On 9 July 1900 they came to Bognor for the dual purpose of opening the Victoria Convalescent Home and Princess Mary Memorial Home

GOD BLESS YOUR PRESENCE AT BOGNOR

Sussex Turnpikes

159 Southerham Gate and toll-house, near Lewes, 1865. The South Street, South Malling-Longbridge, Alfriston Trust was set up in 1759 and this gate introduced in 1819. Sixty years later, in 1879, it was removed when the trust expired

160 Lindfield Toll-gate in High Street, 1870's. This was set up under the Newchapel–Brighthelmston Turnpike Trust of 1770 which expired in 1884. On 31 October in that year the gate was dismantled to be burnt in the High Street on 5 November

161 East Grinstead Gate, 1864. Controlled by the City of London–East Grinstead Trust established in 1717, the toll-gate was at the then southern entrance to the town. The trust was wound up about 1865 and the gate removed soon afterwards. The toll-house was the low building at the left

162 Petworth Gate, by Union House, North Street, *c.* 1870. The Petworth Trust, which controlled 28 miles and 6 furlongs of road in Surrey and Sussex, was established in 1757 and extinguished on 1 May 1877. The building with dormer windows was the poorhouse. The village school *(extreme right)* was destroyed by bombs on 29 September 1942

163 The opening of the Bognor branch line, 1 June 1864: the first train about to leave Barnham Junction. It was headed by 2–2–2 locomotive No. 29, with 5 ft 6 ins driving wheels, built by Sharp

The Railway

164 A stationary train at Eastbourne, 1868. Engine No. 230, 0–4–2. This ran frequently in both directions between Eastbourne and Polegate, merely as a link with the main Hastings–Lewes service at the old Polegate station

165 The Mayfield railway accident, 1 September 1897, 17 years to the day after this line opened in 1880. On the curved section between Heathfield and Mayfield the train was derailed near Clayton Farm, the driver being killed. The six coaches were headed by D tank-class engine, Bonchurch

166 Horsham old station, *c.* 1859. The railway reached Horsham from Three Bridges on 14 February 1848, and was extended to Petworth on 15 October 1859. The work seen in progress may have been occasioned by this extension

167 Hassocks Gate station, up platform, in the 1870's. It was here that the first permanent rail of the London and Brighton railway was laid on 4 February 1839. The station entrance was formerly about 100 yards further north than the present one. The name was changed to Hassocks station on 1 October 1881

168 The up platform at Worthing station, period the late 1860's. The Brighton to Shoreham line was extended to Worthing on 24 November 1845. The station platforms were offset, the other being west of the foot crossing. The bridge was built in 1852 and has been rebuilt and widened recently

169 Petworth, a trim country station, 1889: the top-hatted stationmaster and his staff. Seven years after the railway reached Petworth it was extended to Midhurst, on 15 October 1866. The station closed in 1955, but the line was used for goods traffic until 1966, after which the rails were lifted

170 Stationmaster and staff at Lewes station. It is thought that this group is at the original station in Friars Walk (1846–1857), which was the terminus of the line from Brighton. If not, they are certainly at the second station, a through one, opened on 1 November 1857 and used until the present station was built in 1889